Praise for Cloudshade

Early in Cloudshade, *the speaker in "Far Between Towns" declares that "Only the wind and its music / remember this place." But that makes Lori Howe's poems like the wind's music, because they remember to the reader this place, the high plains, in all its many voices: the voices of those "wild prophets," the coyotes; the voice of rain after a long dry spell pouring off roofs onto "ground / cracked and brittle as an old boot"; the voice of ice "cracking like gunshot".... These are poems set "to fill our mouths / with the earth's own tongue."*
—H. L. Hix , author of *God Bless, Lines of Inquiry*, and *I'm here to learn to dream in your language*

In Cloudshade: Poems of the High Plains, *Lori Howe gives song to landscapes abandoned and unadorned, places where "wind has erased its hieroglyphs." Whether shadowed by ghosts, weather, or the fragility of love, Howe staves off loss with precise and vivid language. Her voice is "mineral and granite" enriched by "a gracious plenty of color." Her powerful poems are mercy and light.*
—Alyson Hagy, author of *Snow, Ashes, Graveyard of the Atlantic*, and *Boleto: A Novel*

As we read Lori Howe's wonderful collection, Cloudshade: Poems of the High Plains, *we discover what the poet, W.H. Auden, called, "Topophilia," a sudden encounter with the landscape. When landscape becomes more than mere geography, and more than mere reflection of a speaker, we find in this collection, due to Howe's diligence, places of beauty and disaster, and the poems become a testament of these places where "there is no marker / cast in bronze, / only the empty stare / of gin bottles, / curled leather boots, / and shards of sapphire tiles /*

left to mimic the sky." Within these poems, place reminds us of the unrelenting nature of time, and our fleeting human lifespan within the long reality of life in the harsh high plains, but if we read these poems close enough, we will also unearth evidence of hope, of how we endure.
–Lindsay Wilson, author of *No Elegies*

In Lori Howe's Cloudshade *we are presented with the seasons of a Wyoming year beginning in an unusually dry June, the earth pulling in on itself. The year passes with the coyotes' distant call, the dark of a prairie bar and its human inhabitants born "...neon blue/and feet first/into a field of summer/ harmonicas." Then there is the rain that falls from the clouds but dries before it hits the ground, the empty houses and towns, the railroad sidings abandoned and rotting, everything that is lost and--by most people—forgotten. And no matter the season there's always a storm brewing somewhere not far away. With the return of spring in the collection's last section, the rain finally arrives and the pronghorn antelope graze on the green grasslands but it's a brief time of plenty in a land that we learn was never meant for humans, "never meant to host a softness/ of bodies."*
–David Romtvedt, author of *Wyoming Fence Lines, Some Church,* and *Certainty*

In Cloudshade, *the language is graceful and luminous, and through Howe's eyes we see railroad towns, animals, weather, and the ghosts of the past, and experience landscape and geography in thrilling ways. Her poems make you feel deeply connected to place—and our place—in the natural world.*
–Nina McConigley, author of *Cowboys and East Indians*

Cloudshade

Cloudshade

Poems of the High Plains

Lori Howe

Sastrugi Press
San Diego • Jackson Hole

Sastrugi Press / Published by arrangement with the author

Cloudshade: Poems of the High Plains

Sastrugi Press
2907 Iris Avenue, San Diego, CA 92173, United States
www.sastrugipress.com

Library of Congress Catalog-in-Publication Data
Library of Congress Control Number: 2015948367
Howe, Lori
Cloudshade / Lori Howe - 1st United States edition
p. cm.
1. Poetry 2. Poetry—American 3. Poetry—Women Authors
Summary: The poems of Cloudshade breathe with the vivid, fragrant essence of life in every season on America's high plains.
ISBN-13: 978-0-9960206-9-5
ISBN-10: 0-9960206-9-1

821.08'

Printed in the United States of America

Cover painting: Lillegraven, Linda. *Path*. 1995. Oil on linen. Private collection.
www.lindalillegraven.com

10 9 8 7 6 5 4 3 2 1

For Erik, Kimberly, Leif, and Jasmine

and in loving memory of Anna Stong Bourgeois, who so loved the high plains

Table of Contents

Acknowledgments

Grateful thanks to the following publications who first published these poems:

Amistad Poetry: "Plum Sky"
Blue Light: "Midnight Gospel"
Clerestory Poetry Journal: "High Plains Solstice"
Gamut's Northern Front: "Beach Camping, Nebraska"
Open Window Review: "At the Bottom of the Lake," "On the Ice"
Owen Wister Review: "Los Rosalia, Olivares"
Pilgrimage: Story, Spirit, Witness, Place: "Rain Coming—for B.H. Fairchild"
Salt Glass: "The Mercies of April"
The Meadow: "En Route to My Father's Funeral"

Sequencing Though Time and Place: Ucross/London/Fort Laramie. Wendy Lemen Bredehoft, Susan Moldenhauer, and Margaret Wilson, (Eds.). "Ghosts of the High Plains."

With deepest appreciation of the Wyoming Arts Council for their financial investment in Individual Artist Development, the University of Wyoming English Department and College of Education for research and travel support, and the Jackson Hole Writers Conference and the Wyoming Humanities Council for their continued support of the arts in Wyoming.

Infinite thanks, also, to fellow workshop poets and writing companions Jason Deiss, Heather Gallardo, Sunnie Gaylord and Oscar Lilley, and to Alyson Hagy, Harvey Hix, Nina McConigley, David Romtvedt, Lee Ann Roripaugh, and Lindsay Wilson for the grace and generosity of their words.

Eternal thanks to my family: Erik, Kim, Leif, and Jasmine, for love, humor, and patience.

For rivers of inspiration, many thanks to B. H. Fairchild, Eric Shaffer, Diane LeBlanc, E. Annie Proulx, and Anthony Doerr.

Infinite gratitude and admiration to Aaron Linsdau and the extraordinary staff at Sastrugi Press.

I stand between the blue of summer and the lake
    of forgetting, the gauze of cells sheathing my hands

empty of everything but traceries,
    the upward gaze of daisies submerged in cold water,

a fish's silver fin, the familiar bend and ache.

"One Hundred and One"
Eric Shaffer
Tony A. Alcantara
Matt Daly

Summer

Rain Coming—For B. H. Fairchild

All that June,
we stood on sidewalks
and on the prairie,
in front and backyards,
outside the hardware store,
in furrows and corrals,
looking skyward, all of us,
as though actors
in an apocalyptic film,
waiting for a meteor
to knock the very earth
from her axis.

It felt like that;
not the rain
we awaited,
but its absence.

In the always-wet month of June,
the prairies withered,
heat-scorched as August.
Only virga teased the air
between earth and clouds,
and the high plains
became an ossuary
for sad, brittle bones,
the newborn of the wild herds

too small
to weather the heat,
to reach the secret, wet places.

All across the high plains,
ranchers lay awake at night,
staring into drought-dark
nothing,
the scent of failure
humming close
like the memory of locusts.

In town, too, we stood
tasting the air for water,
reading the patterns of leaves
turned up in the wind,
the direction of birds,
myopic stages of the moon.

All around us,
the west caught fire.
And held it.

From skies opaque
with smoke,
ash fell onto our porches
and into our hands
as we stared skyward,
praying for rain.

July:
a bare smattering at first,
not enough to wet a sidewalk, really,
dark, bitter jewels that broke hard
and meant nothing.
Then, a graceful glaze
on windows,

tracing down to the open mouth
of the land,
came into its full self
all at once, pouring off roofs
and pooling on ground
cracked and brittle as an old boot...
a slow and grateful
sinking in.

Five weeks of rain.
Rain in August—
daily rain. Rain ankle-deep
in the street,
rain in gutters, rain on hats,
rain on telephone wires
and bare feet,
on tractors
and laundry forgotten
on the line,
glad, shining rain
turning everything,
everything,
into its richer self,

and the prairie green
as spring
and flung with flowers.

Even later, with the heat broken,
when the afternoons darken
and the rain comes in,
we stop talking, put down our pencils
and tools
and thoughts,

walk away, outside,
to watch it,
the feathered sweep of wet fingers
over the mountains,
an easy, lavender falling,
so dear to us that we scarcely dare
to trust rain now.

Like love,
we have known ourselves
without it,
wanting vainly to close our hands
around something precious
that cannot be held.

Beach Camping, Nebraska

Seagulls skreek their Evensong,
sailing updrafts,
dipping to lavender edges,
luminous eyes and beaks
seeking crayfish
and minnows.

Sensing nightfall,
hearing the gulls from down here,
beetles make glittered wings
out of sand
and trace blind paths
in the darkness.

Whipping home on audible wings,
the gulls coast south,
fluting sunset's copper lines
with silver streaks,
bodies white with lingering sun,
the twilight panfired,
raining blueberried light on sandbars
and a darker turquoise, like music,
out across the water.

Plum Sky

In this dream
I am running,
breathing lightly,
my stride amber
as cornrows, arched
as early wheat
in strong wind.

Sun berths at
the Never summers,
cracks the snow edge,
strafes the sky
a pungent bowl
of violet and copper:
ripe plums
waiting for mouths.

When I wake
I am tired from running,
scoured and thirsty
as a bit of glass left out
on the salt flats,
and I know
that only weakened blood,
pale as fish from too much love,
would claim a purple morning sky
could long for someone's lips.

High Plains Solstice

In this close, dark bar
miles out on the prairie,
we are born neon blue
and feet-first
into a field of summer
harmonicas.

An upright bass of hubcaps
and license plates
thumps us all a hot second
heartbeat,
and four jazz trumpets
ripen electric
in the still-warm air
from doors flung wide
like generous mouths
welcoming the night.

The music carves hot petals
through our bodies
in this ritual of tides
and light;
licks us open
from the inside,
and we are night-blooming
jasmine,
seduced by the moon.

Midnight Gospel

In the cool, fullness of night,
the coyotes come closer,
just out of sight
beyond rocks
and scrub sage.
Their song is mineral,
of cold water and granite.

Elemental as wind,
as blood,
these wild prophets
give me back my own tongue
when I cannot
find it.

In my mind, I can see them—
low-slung bodies and fierce eyes,
coats silvered with moonlight,
heads thrown back,
throats filled with this mournful
purity,
not asking to be saved.

Anniversary

Love is a sieve,
keeps us traveling light.
Blackbirds sing in the raspberry canes,
and beneath their song, this river.

Lady of the Valley

Arms awash in wind
and skirt filled with birds,
this spruce,
ancient and prayerful,
whispers softly
across all seasons,
her internal weather
and deep green heart
giving shelter to the small town
of animals
that nests, unseen, inside her.

Long before the railroad unfolded
streets and buildings
across the Laramie valley,
our placid lady stood in this same place,
a slender girl in a fresh green dress.

Even now, each morning, the sun paints
the eastern range
and runs a golden hand   down her face
in benediction,
anointing her with light.

When the cool pleasures of evening
mist down from the mountains, smoothing us
toward night,
our lady folds emerald hands
over we who dream,
her rosemary breath
soft against our foreheads
both waking and asleep.

Fall

Cloudshade

Out across the sleeping plains
with their wind-smoothed linen,
grey-green, undulant,
the clouds follow a course
of genetic memory,
their shadows reviving
the ghosts of the great herds,
spilling fluidly out in wide arcs,
filling creekbeds and couloirs
with one dark, unending pelt,
flowing toward grazing grounds
that lure them back into the world
of men.

And when the clouds come
with more rain
than they can bear,
they gauze down with virga
or glaze the cracked plains
with what cannot long
be held,
and the creeks run a burnt red,
calling
welcome home,
welcome home.

Tangible Stretch—Royal Gorge, CO

I wonder how you build
a bridge that has nothing
to rest on,
nothing reaching up in support only
cables
stretching away.

Who slides the first tangible
across the chasm, makes air
divide around desire?

It must be
daring,

vivid as the first scent
of an orange,

drawn in our blood
like a secret map,
that brings all that is possible

home.

Far Between Towns

A stagecoach stop,
a mercantile....
this collection of deep-grooved boards
so nearly gone, wind has erased
its hieroglyphs.
Too big for a house,
far from any road,
it wards its secrets
in silence.

The steps have all split
and fallen,
fanned like an old hand of cards
beneath the sun-shot porch.
All around, a scattering
of two-penny nails
like dark mushrooms.

New arms of willow
grow within the walls,
and windows hold scraps
of raveled curtain and wavering grass.
From within, a view of the Never Summers;

from without, climbing leaves
as light and fragile
as green glass.

Wind combs through the sage
and rifles the pockets

of black walnut trees
for their green, round fruit—
at the center of their density,
hard nuts like hidden coins—
strange as peacocks
on these old-maid plains.

Only the wind and its music
remember this place,
waiting to own it
when it has at last
outlived everyone
who ever knew it was here.

Reading Maps at Night

At night,
when I can smell your skin
as we sleep,
vast, salty lakes and cities
and roads across mountains
easily fit in the millimeter's space
between your body and mine.

Here, dreams are fissures
in gneiss rock
where the things we fear to name
in daylight
can be dropped and caught,
like mercury,
separating and rolling back
to us
in silver petals,
then perfect spheres.

Offerings

Evening falls
across the neighborhood,
scented with wood smoke
and desire.
Cottonwoods
—archivists of centuries—
lift thousands of creased,
golden pages
to the end of day,
each line of text
darkening inward
toward winter.

At the corner,
the failing light
falls across a pair of shoes
knotted and tossed
over a telephone wire.
They glow white and helpless
as purple-gilled fish,
caught and strung together,
waiting for a biblical rain
to fill the streets
and rise, rise,
to float them free,
unknot them at last
into an alluvial sea.

Dusk

Leaning softly
into the curvature
of seasons,
blackbirds
glide silently
through the gloaming:
feathered scraps
the color of loss,
they open warm, dark hearts
to the coming months
of false night.

Factories Row, Wyoming

You can see them
from town,
the few left to scatter
their belongings
along the rails,
to gradually kneel
beside the river,
waiting for trains
that don't stop here
anymore.

A smudged painting
of some lesser Chicago,
square, dark bodies outlined
with coal dust and sand,
the bitter orange
of creosote,
metal insides
cold enough to burn
your hand.
From a distance,
mullioned eyes
flicker empty panes
like dark moths
in an industrial sky.

At dusk, you can imagine
trains stopping here,
sweating steam, waiting
while their cars fill
with giant metal spools

or tractor rakes,
door knobs
or men's hats,
then rocking backward
to start forward,
heaving their laden bulk
up the rail,
heading further west,
stopping next for a fragrant cargo
of melons ripening
in the violet hour.

In eastern cities,
these factories would live
second lives as offices,
as hip condos, all glass
and stamped ceilings,
tattooed baristas gazing
through the espresso hiss
out those same windows
that workmen once did
while they waited for the whistle
to blow twice for lunch,
three times for emergency,
and four times at day's end.

Here, the hulks by the rails
are a no-man's land of rust,
and the best of them still stand,
doors locked,
walls singing tuneless
in the high plains wind.

They await the return of usefulness,
and in the modest November dusk,
their bones glow a darkening copper
into another unremarkable night.

At the Bottom of the Lake

I slide my small, green boat
into the shallows
as the storm comes in,
autumn thunder cracking
to the west,
the light a strange
pearl
caught between water
and thick-bellied clouds.

Inside this granite bowl,
all is sound and deep gray
shifting
when the wind falls in.

The galoshes
I bought this morning,
too-big and black,
have slashes across the shins
that invite the lake
into the felted hollows
that hold my small feet.

I imagine the man
who owned these boots,
wonder if he still lives,
if he remembers what cut these boots
to uselessness,
not even worth the thrift store dimes

I gave for them, not now,
with the cold, clean lake
cupping my instep
like a ghost.

The surface of the water
is graceful pewter,
many-folded and elegant,
quiet as elephants.
The arc of each wave
catches the small light
and glows,
round and green as an eye.

Weather pulls its string tight,
and the sky gathers in.
Fingers singing,
I ship my paddle, hands in pockets,
close my eyes and am weightless
as lichen.
Even the aspens, still vibrant
in their draws and coves,
huddle together for warmth
as the storm makes us all up
in its secret gray bed.

Los Rosalia, Olivares

1929
Maricarmen Rosalia
leaned from the window
of her kitchen,
breathing in
the steaming land,
the hot dust of the walls,
the wet morning smoke
from her fire,
the feathers of her chickens
in the rain.
She uprooted all the roses
in the graveyard.

Bring everything
to America.

Paloma,
the *gallina* she chose to pack
in a satchel
for the trip across water,
cackled once,
sourly,
inside her cave
of woven husks.

Black eye accusing,
she spat an egg
uncrackable as any stone
to spite the woman—
Maricarmen had cut

the necks of every hen
and rooster
and chick,
leaving Paloma her spotted wings
speckled by the blood of her young
like a flag of insurrection.
She would cluck only once,
a hot September day,
scratching in dirt
brought by sack
from Andalucía.
In the sun, for a moment,
she forgot her stains.

Dirt,
being dirt, was less bitter.
Inert detritus of a garden
left behind,
the soil held its remnants
of rain,
eggshells
and ashes,
it forced down
the contractions
of seeds,
and waited.

Maricarmen
carried another satchel,
slept with it in her arms,
opened it once a day
to touch the seeds
of her house.
Her husband claimed

by post
that the soil
of Wyoming
would take their seeds,
grow children and olives,
chickens and grapes.
It would leave the scent of rain
on walls.

She brought the roses
ground to powder
in a jar.
Calm on the heaving deck,
She watched clouds
on a pan-fired sea.
It seemed right to her,
the roses casked
like wine
for the journey.

Reaping

Ranchers
thought western cattle
could weather on nothing.
The starving animals
ate the green promise
of olives and grapes,
and died anyway.

Another season
brought a harvest
and the birth of a son.

The death of a husband.

Locusts.

2015
Walking
the western edge
of this town
with my dog,
I find a house
that streets
formed around,
walls like chestnut
honey,
grown there from seeds
carried on a woman's back
across the water.

Speckled chickens scratch
in a yard claimed by sage
and wild rose,
the air
from a place
where morning smoke
smells wet
as a downpour.
Through a broken window,
I see the blue
of the Virgin,
fading on the wall:
los Rosalia, Olivares,
olive trees
on a painted tin sign
left leaning against her robes.

Too dry for rust,
the sign remembers
nails, voices,
a harvest in strange soil.

If I could tunnel
under this house,
push through a crack
in the foundation,
I'd find jars of olives
and cellar walls of oiled roots,
I'd find a bowl of water
to conjure a warm rain,
to hold the heavy cinnamon
of a woman's hair
against the hot faces of men,
the lace of dresses,
the scent of births.
I'd find an empty basket
to carry the voices of *los Rosalia,*
a cask of powdered rose
to call their storm
of olives and of brine.

Winter

Winter Archipelago, Vedauwoo

Mindless of time,
these few last mammoths
stood still
until their stories turned
to salt,
written in heat and water
on the inside
of their igneous skins,
before they hardened,
immortal.

In softer seasons,
humans come—
fragile, bright and tiny
as beetles—
to try themselves
against the placid stone.

In winter's quiet,
footed by untouched drifts
and beaver dams closed up tight
against the cold,
Vedauwoo gazes
out across the plains,
a fine gauze of blowing snow
softening the world
back to an ancient sea,
lost to all but these elephant islands
and their long memories of water.

On the Ice

Dusk crosses
slender blue wrists
over the lake.
Fishermen
with augers
and bright jackets
haul away fishhuts
weathered as silver mines
from the Sierra Madres.

Clouds of fogged breath
lace around the men
as they load pickup beds
with full iceboxes.
Inside them,
sleek, scaled bodies,
yet breathing, twine together,
delaying death
with their fiercest heat.

Tail lights recede,
disappear.
The lake reclaims its hush,
begins to speak
in nightvoice,
whaletongue,
and we slide out

onto the pebbled eyelid
of ice, cold coming through
our thickest socks and boots.

We wait, silent, hearing with our feet
the seething of ultramarine blood,
the twitching of bones,
rumbles of omens
and restless spirits.
The ice stretches and heaves,
cracking like gunshot,
and beneath that, glints and gleamings
of sound, like whales
calling across the darkness.

And we, small minutes of soft flesh
and clacking teeth, stand perfectly still,
as though we might translate
this tectonic music
into some hoped-for message
from a generous God.

Mending

My grandfather mended fence
in the cold light of Januaries.

He mended with other lined men
in heavy jackets
and leather gloves stiff with frost.
Amongst them, gestures,
few words,
the upward thrust of a chin—
enough language
for the task.

My mother's grandfather mended net
in the cold rain of mornings by the sea.

He mended with other lined men
in rubber boots
and oilskin jackets
as the sky slicked down their necks
and across chests and backs
strong from pulling nets
and mending them.

They mended fence and net with your
grandfather
and your mother's grandfather
without speaking
and knew each other's minds
through the movement of their hands.

I would mend with you
on the plains or on wet rocks by the sea,
but our hands are empty now—
you cannot know my mind
by watching me,
you cannot know me by the sharpness
of my blade or needle,
you cannot tell my heart
by the clean motion of my knots.

Ghost Houses

All across the plains,
you'll find them—
these houses look fine,
a little worn,
like any place people live,
but the curtains are tattered,
permanently open,
and the shingles
trail each other
off the roof
like squirrels.

The walls are dirt-stained
to the knees, all red.

Inside,
lamps fan out in broken wings
of glass,
a couch has lost its footing,
sprawls unconscious
on the floor.
A box of letters
has swollen and burst,

handwriting intimate,
unfamiliar.

Corners fill with things
left unsaid.
The kitchen waits:
table set for breakfast,

kettle on the stove,
maple syrup bottle
fading in the sun.
There are coffee grounds
on the counter,
lemon soap beside the sink,
a work coat
astride the back of a chair.

Time has rotted,
swallowed by moths,
and dust is what the years have bred.
Spiders embroider lace
on a forgotten dress,
and winter has slept in the bed.
These houses do not know
that they are dead.

Twilight and Dawn

I wake each morning
in the half darkness
of moon filtered through trees.
The moon is unconcerned by states
that I always take personally—
it knows fullness and lack
are guiltless and temporary,
knows not to privilege one
or lament the other.

Dawn is a violet poem
I have memorized,
twilight its translation
on the opposite page.

In the blue shadow of morning
the sky is a lavender envelope
into which I fit perfectly;
no differentiation between my body
and bare cottonwoods, granite,
frost-flocked wheat.

If you could look a thousand miles
to where I stand in the Laramie dawn,
if you looked with all your breath
you'd see a faint outline of woman,
lupine-colored, a patch cut from morning,
leaning into day as though growing
toward you.

The Eight

The wooden cross
is rough beneath my hand,
as eight pairs
of running shoes
turn in the wind
like chimes struck
silent
by grief.
They would be fathers
now,
these lost sons
of the high plains.

Up the road,
someone lights candles
in the windows of their house,
and faintly comes
the tin sound
of a radio playing
in the barn,
the mismatched voices
singing some old song
I want suddenly,
terribly,
to recognize.

En Route to My Father's Funeral

I leave the Interstate
for a probable future
of map-wrestling
in the weak dome light,
and the Kansas moon stands up
to look at me.

Silvered against it,
I feel a stray atom
from when we were all
still fish
twitch inside my bones.

All highways
head straight across Kansas—
long, quiet stretches,
the darkened arches of roofs.
I imagine the people asleep
in their beds,
and they wrap their blankets tight
inside me, turning over,
breathing deep.

At a pale crossroads,
in an open shop two floors up,
a welder works into the night.
His arc is lonesome in the cool air,

gobbets of fire
like unformed angels
falling.

As a child,
I watched this same
mercurial rain
from my father's shop—
strange hobby, I'd thought,
for the silent man
who shared my own eyes,
my own wrists—
not knowing his fire
would buy my clothes
and shoes,
come autumn.

In the rearview mirror,
I arch to see the last drops
leap away.
Strange, I tell
the sleeping Kansans,
this aching,
this longing for a life
I swear I never loved.

Spring

The Mercies of April

I walk home
in the deepening of 6pm,
through shadows that fill
the wells
of my footprints
with amethyst thoughts.
Overhead,
pigeons on telephone
cables sway iridescently—
glad, warm bundles
of pewter
and blue,
they give back
the afternoon light
like a gift.

Along my path,
winter has turned out
its pockets,
and the scraps and trinkets
of lives,
things we've lost,
poke their fingers
through the snow.

Most of what surfaces
in false spring
awakens too soon—
bird bones, white and graceful
as letters in lost languages,
swollen pages

of drowned books,
broken glass,
unsoftened by time—
they all wait
for the snows of April
to come back,
pull a clean, heavy sheet
over them,
give them time
to disappear,
to find their way
back to sea.

Under the cover of dusk,
we all await this grace:
an angle of repose,
a green unfolding
of our softer selves,
inside the chill
white hands
of this dark,
high plains spring.

New Trees—for Courtney Westhoff

I hover at the door,
one foot outside,
as the friend I have called
to evaluate some love-child
aspen trees
eyes them up and down,
assessing the damage
they have already done
and are likely to do
to my foundation.

I want to move them,
slim bendable wisps
like skinny, fair little girls
with their pale hair trembling
in the slightest breeze.
I want to save them,
move them nearer the mother
that cast them here,
let them put down fresh roots
and thrive.

My friend shakes his head,
one small gesture
of futility,
and I know it's hopeless;
their root systems have shaken out
into sap-filled cords,
have seeped like piano music
under my foundation,
and will die if I move them.

They are just saplings,
six slender, grey-white bodies
against the house,
their leaves,
translucent, citrine,
no larger than my thumb.
I feel silly at my grief,
as though they were children
or horses,
their thin bark
a tender skin or pelt
meant to hold them together.

My friend has brought his axe,
but before he pulls it
from its old leather chock,
not knowing I can see him,
he lays his big, rough hand
against each small tree,
pressing it there for just a moment,
telling them each a story
that can only be heard
through osmosis.

When my friend has cut them down—
the work of 5 minutes—
he carries them easily to his truck
and lays them in the bed.
The real work begins then,
with the sharp edge of a shovel,
as he slices through roots
and hauls them out, one by one.
"You can't leave the roots,"
he says to no one,

“there’s no point in cutting trees
if you don’t take the roots.”

I imagine whole houses undermined
with roots that stayed hidden
when trees were removed,
how they ache like phantom limbs
of amputees,
useless and attached to nothing
but memory,
invisible hands and fingers clenched,
long after all visible traces of them
have gone.

Before the Rain

In the shadows of early morning
the sparrows return,
beaks full of grass and slender twigs,
to reinforce the homes they've built
inside our rain pipes.
Their chicks learn to fly inside these pipes.
Like children on scooters,
they whir from east to west along the house,
flapping furiously, unafraid,
longing for the open sky
but protected still, cupped in a thin metal skin
meant to channel rain.

For a week, we paused beneath the gutters,
ears cocked,
wondering at the odd confluence
of cross-breeze
that could make the pipes hum like that,
a sound caught somewhere between a dog's
snore
and the thrum of a chain-link fence
whisked with a stick.
And then, we saw them—
tiny yellow heartbeats,
fierce, joyful eyes,
the fluff of feathers scant protection
against the angular mountain spring.

Beaks wide, they demand
the return of the harried parents,
the last bits and bugs and worms

they won't catch for themselves.
From inside the house, we watch,
and begin to worry about rain.
For it is time for rain,
for big, round, heavy rain tinged indigo
with snow,
for a rain that will sweep away the downy nest
and our unexpected tenants
in one long swallow.
We silently agree to rig something,
some slight cover, something to divert the
river
from our tiny charges, before it comes.

We are too slow, though;
the next day begins in tumult,
and we wake to a symphony of water
crashing percussive
against the window.
We are too late, we think,
but we run, anyway, fetch a ladder,
watch for tiny settlements to wash out, ruined
and silent, on the drenty ground.

But there is nothing—no tiny bodies, no
Worst Fears Realized.
They knew.
Weather is no news to sparrows;
rain and its schedules are written inside
them
in a language we ourselves have long forgotten,
and they kept to that safety just long
enough,
just as long as was necessary,
and then, without sorrow,
without regret,
they left us.

Shirley Basin Road

My hand on the wheel,
you lean out the window
to shoot a herd
of camera-shy antelope,
their tawny legs fluid,
elegant,
as they abandon the road
for secret places
we'll never know.

We're humming through
this spring-green veldt
on a disused stretch of tarmac
cracked and lined as elephants,
serpentine troughs
in the draws and lees.

Dropping into Bates Hole,
prairie hollows fill silver
with handfuls of sky,
and a straggle of burnt timbers
stands still
against a braille
of greasewood and sage:
a calendar of The Bad Years.

Closer to town,
Hereford calves
and fields of purple clover
lift glad faces
to quick scraps of May sun,

and along this rotted shipwreck
of a road,
ditches quicken with yellow flowers
and the green singing
of a thousand frogs.

Apocrypha

One busy June night,
a train derailed
where the river bends south,
crushing one of the whorehouses
and everyone inside,
the fire hot enough
to fuse metal and bone.

There is no marker
cast in bronze,
only the empty stare
of gin bottles,
curled leather boots,
and sherds of azure tiles
left to mimic the sky.

Ghosts of the High Plains

In afternoon light,
golden stones stack skyward,
the thorned hands of the plains
holding them up.

Beyond their scant shelter,
the mineral spine of the prairie
stretches
to meet the wind,
and only small jewels
of prairie glass
and odd metal findings
mark this place in any way
human.

Such land,
never meant to host a softness
of bodies,
the hunger and thirst
of blood and skin.
A gracious plenty of color—
of scouring wind and heat,
and of beauty enough
to fill our mouths
with the earth's own tongue.

Inside the Night Sky—for Anthony Doerr

We live between two luminous bodies—
ancient rivers beneath us,
and above, a cathedral turning liquid,
a nightly creek running high
with prayer.
All the light we cannot see
comes back to us by midnight,
a warm surrounding,
a clouded, phosphorescent sea.

Held fast to the deserts
and mountains, we settle
this space between moon
and water, heart and mind.
There are no roads to the center
of either universe,
no maps to clarify
such heavenly journeys.

At last, we lie down like buffalo,
to follow the inscriptions
in our blood.
We merge into darkness,
hoping our souls will rise
to that far, gleaming place
where dreams go
when we open our eyes.

About the author

Lori Howe is the author of *Cloudshade: Poems of the High Plains* (Satrugi Press, 2015), *Voices at Twilight: A Poet's Guide to Wyoming Ghost Towns* (Elm Books, 2016), and *Stories from Earth: Millennials, Literature,* and *Teaching Writing that Matters*. Her poems, short fiction, and non-fiction appear in numerous journals, anthologies, and books such as *The Meadow, Pilgrimage, Northern Lights, Red Hook, Open Window Review, Frontiers Magazine,* and the *Owen Wister Review*. She holds undergraduate and graduate degrees in English and Spanish, as well as an M.F.A. in poetry from the University of Wyoming.

She is currently a doctoral candidate in Literacy Studies at the University of Wyoming, where she teaches in the College of Education, serves on the leadership team of the Wyoming Writing Project, and teaches creative writing/literacy workshops with writers around the state. Her research on creative writing workshop pedagogy appears in journals such as the Journal of Lifelong Learning and Qualitative Inquiry. She is the editor in chief of Clerestory: Poems of the Mountain West (clerestorypoets.org), and has appeared as a guest poet on Wyoming Public Radio. Her current writing project is the novel, Heaven of Olives, set in Wyoming, New York City, and Andalucía, Spain.

Lori lives in Laramie, Wyoming.

Enjoy other Sastrugi Press titles

Journeys to the Edge by Randall Peeters, PhD.

Ever wonder what it's like to climb Mount Everest? The idea isn't as far-fetched as it may seem, even though very few people in the world have climbed Mount Everest. It requires dreaming big and creating a personal vision to climb the mountains in your life. Randall Peeters shares his guidelines to create a personal vision.

These Canyons Are Full of Ghosts by Emmett Harder

Driven to find his fortune in the most desolate and forbidding landscapes on earth, one prospector learns there is more to finding gold than just using a shovel and pickaxe. While exploring the massive national park, Emmett Harder crosses paths with Death Valley's most notorious resident: Charles Manson.

The Blind Man's Story by J.W. Linsdau

Imagine one's surprise to be hiking in the great Northwest and coming across someone who is blind and spends his summers living high on a mountain. That's what happened to journalist Beau Larson. He returns to work to cover a dispute between local timber workers and environmentalists. Beau finishes his report, but soon discovers there is more to the story than he thought.

Antarctic Tears by Aaron Linsdau

What would make someone give up a high-paying career to ski across Antarctica alone? This inspirational true story will make readers both cheer and cry. Fighting skin-freezing temperatures, infections, and emotional breakdown, Aaron Linsdau exposes harsh realities of the world's largest wilderness. Discover what drives someone to the brink of destruction while pursing a dream.

Prevailing Westerlies by Ed Lavino

With clarity and intensity Lavino's photographs express longing for the natural world and hope for its future. An intimacy with the Rocky Mountain West born of long familiarity and close observation is evident. These beautiful black and white images are timeless, yet decidedly modern. This artist's unconventional intellect and offbeat perspective will transfix and delight.

Roaming the Wild by Grover Ratliff

Jackson Hole is home to some of the most iconic landscapes in North America. In this land of harsh winters and short summers, wildlife survive and thrive. People from all around the world travel here to savor both the rare vistas of the high Rockies and have the chance to observe bear, moose and elk. It is an environment like no other, covered in snow most of the year yet blanketed by wildflowers for a few precious months. This place is both powerful and delicate.

CPSIA information can be obtained
at www.ICGtesting.com
Printed in the USA
FSOW01n0118110116
15503FS

9 780996 020695